FIFE EDUCATION
COMMITTEE

KING'S ROAD P. SCHOOL
ROSYTH

Summer

Nicola Baxter

Illustrated by Kim Woolley

FRANKLIN WATTS
LONDON • NEW YORK • SYDNEY

In springtime, everything is growing and changing.
As spring ends, the days become warmer.
Slowly, summer arrives.

Now try this
How can you tell that this is a summertime picture?

3

In summer, the sun shines and the days grow longer.
It is still light when it is time to go to bed.

Try this later
Bright sunlight makes shadows.
Stand in the playground early in the morning and
ask a friend to draw round your shadow with chalk.
Do the same thing at midday, standing in the same
place. How has your shadow changed?

Among the summer flowers,
insects fly and settle.
They find food in the flowers and
leaves and make it possible for the
plants to grow fruits and seeds.

The summer sun helps the fruits and seeds to ripen.
Then there is plenty for birds, animals and us to eat.

Grass grows very quickly too.
Gardeners have to mow the grass
every few days to keep it short.

Try this later

How many games and sports can you think of
that are played outside on the grass in summer?
What do you like to play?

In the summer it may not rain very much.
Plants that need plenty of water
may need watering.

Warm summer days make it fun to
be outside.
You can play outside and eat outside.
Some people even sleep outside!

Often the sun is so hot in the summer that you have to be careful.
How can you make sure that the sun does not burn you?

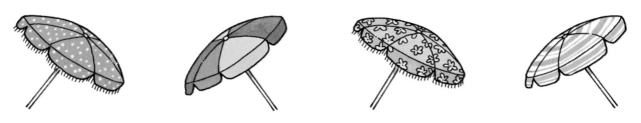

Try this later
Draw a picture of things you like to do to keep cool.

17

Lots of people have a holiday in the summer.
They might stay at home or they might take a trip to somewhere new.

Try this later

What did you do on your last summer holiday?
Make a collection of postcards that your friends
and family have sent you from their holidays.
Where were they from?

While some people are taking a holiday, many farmers are working hard.
When all the crops are ripe, it is time to harvest them.

As the summer ends, the days slowly become cooler again. Autumn is on its way.

23

Index

© 1996 Watts Books

Watts Books
96 Leonard Street
London EC2A 4RH

Franklin Watts Australia
14 Mars Road
Lane Cove NSW 2066

ISBN: 0 7496 2338 1

10 9 8 7 6 5 4 3 2 1

Dewey Decimal Classification
Number 574.5

A CIP catalogue record for this
book is available from the British
Library.

Printed in Malaysia

Editor: Sarah Ridley
Designer: Kirstie Billingham
Picture researcher: Sarah Moule

The publishers would like to thank
Carol Olivier and the pupils of
Kenmont Primary School for their
help with the cover for this book.

Photographs: Bubbles 3, 14; Bruce
Coleman Ltd 4, 7, 18; Frank Lane
Picture Agency 13; Peter Millard
(cover); Natural History
Photographic Agency 8; TRIP 10;
ZEFA 20-21, 23.

24